BBC Gardeners' World

POCKET PLANTS

CLEMATIS

Andi Clevely

Photographs by Jo Whitworth

D0240943

Author Biography

Andi Clevely has been a working gardener for nearly thirty years. He began his career in Leeds City Council central nurseries and since then has worked in many gardens around the country, including Windsor Great Park. He is now responsible for a country estate and large garden in Stratford-on-Avon where he lives with his family. Andi has written a number of gardening books and is a regular columnist for *Homes & Gardens* magazine.

Acknowledgements

The publishers would like to thank Sheila Chapman Clematis Nursery & Garden, Chelmsford; Mike and Dorothy Brown, Clematis Corner, Oxfordshire; Royal National Rose Society, St Albans, Hertfordshire; Treasures of Tenbury, Burford House, Worcestershire and Mrs D. Anderson, West Sussex for their assistance with the photography. All photographs © BBC.

More Information

If you have difficulty finding any of the clematis listed in this book contact The British Clematis Society, The Tropical Bird Gardens, Rode, Bath, Somerset, BA3 6QW, (01373) 830326.

Published by BBC Books,
an imprint of BBC Worldwide Publishing.
BBC Worldwide Limited, Woodlands,
80 Wood Lane, London W12 0TT.

First published 1997
© BBC Worldwide Limited 1997
The moral right of the author has been asserted

ISBN 0 563 38775 0

Photographs by Jo Whitworth

Set in Futura

Printed and bound in Belgium by Proost NV
Colour separations by Radstock Reproductions Limited, Midsomer Norton, Avon
Cover printed in Belgium by Proost NV

Clematis Flowering Times

INTRODUCTION

Clematis is one of the most popular and rewarding garden plants, so numerous and varied in appearance and habit that a variety can usually be found for virtually any position or aspect in the garden. Also, by choosing carefully it is possible to have them in flower virtually all the year round.

The majority are climbers, some so exuberant they will scramble to the top of tall trees, while others are dwarf and ideal for gracing a rock garden; there is also a small group of lovely herbaceous types that grow as non-climbing shrubs. Some varieties have masses of tiny dainty flowers, while others have blooms as large as plates, 20cm (8in) or more across.

Most clematis are deciduous or hardy, although a few are evergreen or even tender, best grown on a warm wall or under glass. Few are difficult to care for, and if grown well they will prove long-lived.

Choosing a site

Match a chosen variety to the space available. Some, such as the *montanas*, for example, are very vigorous and need hard trimming back to fit comfortably into a small garden, whereas many other hybrids grow to a more restrained 1.8–2.4m (6–8ft). Check whether a variety needs full sun or accepts light shade, and also if it is hardy enough for your local climate: *alpinas* withstand harsher weather than *montanas*, for example. (See indivividual entries for requirements.)

Flowering seasons vary widely, and it is worth deciding if you want a spectacular display of colour early or late in the season, or a steady sequence of blooms throughout the summer. Site them where they can be seen clearly, where the fragrance of some

varieties and the fluffy seedheads of others are easily appreciated. And remember that clematis are highly adaptable – as supreme companion plants, they will happily twine up a climbing rose or scramble over an adjacent shrub, and you can grow many varieties in large containers.

Preparing the ground

Most kinds of soil are suitable, provided they are not waterlogged – clematis like good drainage, especially in winter – and are neither very acid nor extremely alkaline. Very heavy or light soils should be dug deeply and fortified with plenty of garden compost or well-rotted manure.

Planting

Clematis are usually supplied pot-grown and can be planted at any time, although spring is the best season. Space them 60cm (2ft) apart when planting two or more together, and 45–60cm (18–24in) away from walls, where the soil tends to be dry in summer.

- Dig out a large hole to accommodate the rootball comfortably, deep enough to plant it 10cm (4in) deeper that it was in the pot (this improves the chances of recovery if the plant wilts).

- Water the clematis, allow to drain, and then remove from its pot but leave the support cane in position. If the roots are tightly coiled at the bottom, carefully tease some free and spread them out in the hole.

- Lean the plant towards its support and replace the soil around the rootball, firming it in place with your foot. Leave the surface slightly hollowed to confine moisture above the roots, and water in well.

- Immediately after planting cut down to about 30cm (12in) above a strong pair of buds to encourage more stems and a bushy plant. Pinch out stems as they grow to stimulate branching.

Care

Watering: Most clematis need plenty of water throughout the growing season, at least 10 litres (2 gallons) every week. Direct water where it is needed by burying a small flower pot or a length of drainpipe beside the plant, and water into this. Shading the roots with a stone slab or adjacent shrub and applying an annual spring mulch help to prevent dryness.

Feeding: Regular liquid feeding every 1–2 weeks during the first year encourages strong early development. Thereafter give an annual mulch of garden compost or well-rotted manure in autumn or spring, spreading it in a circle about 60cm (2ft) wide around the stem Topdress heavy-flowering varieties with general or high-potash fertilizer in spring and mid-summer.

Support: Climbing clematis need support for their twining leaf stems. When grown with host plants such as roses and trees, simply tie in stems to help them start climbing. Elsewhere provide wooden trellis, clematis netting or a network of wires for support. Spread stems out as they grow for even coverage.

Health: Plants are generally trouble-free, and the only serious diseases likely to occur are wilt and mildew.

Clematis wilt is a fungal disease affecting mainly early, large-flowered hybrids. Deep planting, early pinching out to establish a strong stem system, and firm support are sound precautions. If wilt occurs cut plants back to healthy growth, water and feed regularly, and treat with a systemic fungicide. Recovery usually follows immediately, or after 1–2 seasons.

Late, large-flowered clematis, especially white varieties, and hybrids based on *C. texensis* are most at risk from mildew. This usually affects the plants late in the season. They should be sprayed with systemic fungicide as a precaution or treatment, or both.

Pruning

Pruning clematis can seem intimidating and it is often tempting to simply prune immediately after flowering. This is a sound working policy, but some varieties benefit from the more sophisticated treatment summarized here. As explained in the entries, it may be advisable to use a combination of methods to extend or adjust flowering times.

Method 1 Prune after flowering, cutting all side-shoots almost to their base and just above a leaf joint.

Method 2 Minimal pruning, simply cutting off faded flowers above a pair of buds.

Method 3 This offers an option. Either prune lightly after flowering by cutting off faded blooms above a pair of strong buds; or prune hard in late winter or early spring by cutting back all topgrowth to just above the origin of the previous season's growth.

Method 4 Hard prune in late winter or early spring by cutting back all topgrowth almost to the base of the previous season's growth, with one or two main stems occasionally pruned to about 30cm (12in) high to rejuvenate growth.

Method 5 Prune hard in late winter or early spring, cutting back topgrowth almost to the origin of the previous season's growth, or allow to scramble unpruned through tall supports such as trees

'Abundance'

The striking colour of its flowers, which are slightly less nodding than others of its type, makes this one of the most conspicuous *viticella* hybrids. The 5cm (2in) flowers are borne in solid masses on the top portions of the stems.

Flowering time: Mid-summer to early autumn.

Height: 3–3.5m (10–12ft)

Habit: Vigorous and very free-flowering, with flowers slightly pendent, showing the pale mauve-pink reverse of their petals. Blooms are borne on current season's growth.

Positioning: Any aspect, but best grown with a lighter background or companion because of the intense colouring of its flowers.

Care: Very easy to grow; hardy and disease resistant.

Pruning: Hard pruning is best, cutting the mass of stems back annually to about 30cm (12in) above the ground in late winter or early spring to encourage new flowering growth.

Useful tips: Try grouping this variety with a soft pink rose such as 'Doctor van Fleet', or a white climbing clematis like *C. flammula*, together with an herbaceous clematis, for example *C. integrifolia* 'Pastel Pink'.

'Alba Luxurians'

Flowering time: Mid-summer to early autumn.

Height: 3–3.5m (10–12ft)

Habit: Vigorous, hardy and free-flowering, with very pendent blooms produced on the current year's stems.

Positioning: Most aspects, sunny or shaded, but semi-shade enhances the green colouring.

Care: A robust, trouble-free variety that needs little special care. Top-dress lavishly with well-rotted manure in spring.

Pruning: Cut hard back in early spring to about 30cm (12in) high to renew growth and prevent all the flowers from appearing only at the top of the tall stems.

Useful tips: It may be contrasted with stronger coloured plants such as red climbing roses ('Parkdirektor Rogers', for example), but also blends well with a purple clematis or purple-leafed shrub such as *Cotinus coggygria* 'Royal Purple'. Try growing to climb on a mauve buddleia.

This is a fascinating *viticella*, that deserves a prominent position. Its beguiling bell-shaped flowers, an opaque and yet translucent white, charm everyone, while the green extensions to the sepals of the earlier flowers are unique.

alpina 'Pamela Jackman'

A graceful, early-flowering hybrid with single rich blue flowers that are comparatively large. Sometimes blooms appear again in autumn, contrasting with the silky seedheads from earlier flowers.

Flowering time: Mid- and late spring, sometimes again in early autumn.

Height: 1.8–2.4m (6–8ft)

Habit: Medium vigour and slender wiry stems, with flowers carried singly on last year's wood.

Positioning: Grows happily in full sun or on a shaded wall, in most soils. Suitable for growing in containers, or for training over a low wall, small shrub or large rock.

Care: Free drainage is important, so dig plenty of grit or similar coarse material into heavier soils to make sure the ground does not lie wet in winter. Manure well in spring.

Pruning: Prune immediately after flowering, trimming the side-shoots of wall-trained plants back to about 15cm (6in) from the wall, others to 60cm (2ft) high above the ground.

Useful tips: This variety may be trained with a later-flowering rose to use the latter's stems as a supporting framework.

Flowering time: Early summer to mid-autumn.

Height: 1.2–1.8m (4–6ft)

Habit: An herbaceous and non-clinging sub-shrub that needs tying in to trellis or wires, or may be allowed to scramble through a strong shrub for support.

Positioning: Full sun or dappled shade, in a sheltered position where the stems are not disturbed by high winds.

Care: If grown against a wall or fence, stems need to be fanned out and tied in as they extend. Little extra care is necessary when grown with a supporting shrub. Mulch with well-rotted manure in autumn immediately after pruning.

Pruning: Very often the longest stems will die back early as a kind of self-pruning, and these can be removed to neaten plants. Cut back completely in late autumn, almost to soil level.

Useful tips: Try planting this hybrid to trail over semi-prostrate conifers.

A lovely new *integrifolia* hybrid with masses of neat 8cm (3in) blooms that appear successively for much of the summer and well into autumn, perhaps the longest season of any clematis. It makes an ideal companion for many shrubs that in return will support the flowering shoots.

Flowering time: Late spring and early summer, often with a repeat in late summer and early autumn.

Height: 1.5–1.8m (5–6ft)

Habit: Moderately vigorous with fairly compact growth.

Positioning: Best in full sun but will tolerate light shade; deserves a prominent position on a wall or fence, although may also be grown with other plants such as climbing roses.

Care: Early training is important to form a good spread of stems. Top-dress liberally in spring with good garden compost or well-rotted manure, and feed at mid-summer to sustain the second flowering.

Pruning: Either prune lightly after the early flush of blooms, cutting back to a pair of buds, or cut hard back in early spring close to the base of the previous year's growth.

Useful tips: Try planting this variety to cover the bare lower stems of climbing roses.

This is spectacular early in the season, flowering about a fortnight later than single varieties with intensely coloured double blooms 15cm (6in) or more across, and contrasting creamy white stamens. The secondary late summer blooms are single but very welcome.

Flowering time: Late spring to late summer, in flushes.

Height: 1.8–2.4m (6–8ft), sometimes less.

Habit: Fairly compact growth, slow at first but more vigorous when plants are established.

Positioning: Full sun or light shade, although a shaded position will help to prevent early fading of the blooms. Ideal for a shaded wall or for growing with dark-leafed shrubs.

Care: A good site is essential, so prepare the ground thoroughly and top-dress lavishly in spring with garden compost or well-rotted manure. Feed with a liquid fertilizer after the first flush of blooms to help sustain the later performance.

Pruning: Train the stems to prevent their tangling, thinning as necessary where trained on walls. Cut out dead or spindly growth in early spring.

Useful tips: Try using this variety to brighten up *Garrya elliptica* and other shrubs with dull foliage.

This is a form of 'Nelly Moser', with very large flowers up to 18cm (7in) across that are deeper in colour and just as eye-catching. Shade enhances the rich colour but may cause some of the first flowers to have a green tinge.

'Bill Mackenzie'

Not every garden has the space for this spectacular clematis, although hard pruning can help to restrain growth. The flowers are large for an *orientalis*, up to 8cm (3in) across, and often cover the stems completely. The large silvery seedheads last well into winter.

Flowering time: Mid-summer to mid-autumn.

Height: 3–6m (10–20ft)

Habit: Robust and vigorous, covering large areas unless pruned. The foliage is rather plain.

Positioning: This variety needs plenty of room and is best grown over large hedges or into tall trees for maximum impact. Position it where the seedheads can be enjoyed in winter.

Care: Very little where plants are allowed to ramble freely. Plants restrained by hard annual pruning benefit from a light mulch of garden compost or well-rotted manure in spring.

Pruning: No pruning necessary if plants are grown naturally. Otherwise cut hard back to about 30cm (12in) from the ground in late winter or early spring.

Useful tips: Check that your plant is raised from a cutting as many are grown from seed and may be variable in colour and vigour. Excellent when combined with a vigorous climbing rose.

Flowering time: Late spring and early summer.

Height: 7–10m (20–30ft) but may be restrained to 4–5m (15ft).

Habit: Very vigorous, almost rampant. Attractive deep purple-bronze foliage.

Positioning: Best grown in full sun on a house wall or covering a shed or garage. May also be grown into large trees. Spring frosts sometimes destroy the flower buds, so do not site in a known frost pocket.

Care: Very easy to grow. Succeeds even in light infertile soil, although growth is more vigorous if plants are mulched in spring.

Pruning: The vines can be left unpruned to grow to their full extent. Otherwise prune hard back to a main framework of branches, cutting the side-shoots almost to their base after flowering.

Useful tips: The ideal variety for growing to mask an eyesore or soften the outlines of a building.

A fine exuberant variety, bred more recently than most other *montana* varieties but already popular for its deep plum-pink semi-double blooms, 5cm (2in) across and borne in great masses for about 3–4 weeks. Easily grown in almost any situation.

campaniflora

Flowering time: Mid-summer to early autumn.

Height: 4.5–7.5m (15–25ft) but may be pruned to smaller dimensions.

Habit: Rampant growth if left unchecked, with slender dainty stems and pretty foliage.

Positioning: A native of Portugal and best grown in a warm sunny position. It can be trained over sheds and other small buildings, or into open trees.

Care: The only attention necessary is usually pruning to limit size.

Pruning: Where space is not a problem, plants can be left to grow naturally. Elsewhere prune hard in late winter near to the base of the previous year's growth. Occasionally some old stems may be cut down to the ground, and plants will grow more strongly after this renewal pruning.

Useful tips: Plants sometimes produce completely white flowers; this is only temporary and more typical of young plants.

This is an elegant plant for all its astonishing vigour. The 2.5cm (1in) nodding flowers are like dainty little bells, almost waxy in texture and glistening inside with a frosted appearance.

'Carnaby'

Flowering time: Late spring and early summer.
Height: 1.8–2.4m (6–8ft)
Habit: Fairly vigorous, with dense compact growth that is easily trained.
Positioning: Partial sun or dappled shade, because the colour fades badly in bright sunlight. The compact growth makes it a perfect choice for growing in large containers.
Care: Train a good system of branches during the first 2 years and feed liberally to sustain the new growth. Thereafter mulch annually in spring with garden compost or well-rotted manure.
Pruning: Prune hard in early spring. In succeeding years prune lightly, trimming side-shoots back to a strong pair of buds after flowers fade, or cut back hard in late winter or early spring.
Useful tips: An excellent variety for brightening up a shady corner, where its colour is protected from the sun.

A fairly recent American hybrid, with very satisfying and compact growth. It is remarkably free-flowering, the raspberry pink blooms reaching 15–20cm (6–8in) across and smothering the stems for several weeks. One of the best varieties for a shaded position.

This winter-flowering clematis is rather special, with its evergreen foliage and unusual nodding flowers, which are about 5cm (2in) across, scented and extravagantly speckled. In most temperate regions it is best grown in a greenhouse or conservatory for protection.

Flowering time: Mid-autumn to mid-winter or early spring.

Height: Up to 5–6m (16–19ft)

Habit: Evergreen and fairly vigorous, with small shiny leaves.

Positioning: On a warm sheltered wall or in a cool conservatory; in very mild districts plants grow well outdoors on shaded walls not exposed to winds.

Care: Plants cannot stand waterlogging: work plenty of grit and coarse materials into heavier soils, or grow in a large container. Top-dress with garden compost annually after flowering, or liquid feed fortnightly during flowering. Watch out for greenfly and other pests under glass.

Pruning: Cut back side-shoots after flowering to just above a leaf joint near their base. Or limit its size by cutting all growth after flowering back to just above the same point each year.

Useful tips: Sub-species *balearica* and 'Wisley Cream' are other good winter-flowering varieties.

Flowering time:	Early or mid-summer to late summer.
Height:	1.8–2.4m (6–8ft)
Habit:	Strong growing, vigorous but compact, and very reliably hardy, with rich green shiny foliage.
Positioning:	Any aspect; colour is particularly intense on a shaded wall. A good choice for container cultivation.
Care:	A very easy variety to grow as it is very healthy and notably wilt-resistant. Dress generously with well-rotted manure in spring and feed container plants fortnightly with a general liquid fertilizer.
Pruning:	Cut back hard in late winter or early spring, almost to the origin of all the previous year's growth and just above a leaf joint. Occasionally prune one or two older stems back to about 30cm (12in) above ground.
Useful tips:	Combines well with an early climbing rose such as 'Francis E. Lester', and with other daintier clematis, for example C. flammula.

One of the most popular large-flowered hybrids ever introduced, growing and flowering with equal enthusiasm in most situations. The flowers are a wonderfully clear pink, very uniform, and often 15cm (6in) across, making a spectacular display.

'Daniel Deronda'

While the earliest flowers are often semi-double, this variety soon settles down to producing its 20cm (8in) single blooms over the rest of a long season. The suggestion of an ivory stripe down the centre of each flower petal neatly sets off the creamy white stamens.

Flowering time: Late spring or early summer to late summer.

Height: 2.4–3m (8–10ft)

Habit: Despite its height this is a moderately vigorous variety, easily pruned to limit its size.

Positioning: Full sun or very light shade – avoid very shady aspects and positions exposed to cold winds which often damage the top growth. May also be grown in large containers.

Care: Prepare the soil well before planting, and top-dress generously in spring with well-rotted manure. Feed with liquid general fertilizer during the flowering season for later blooms.

Pruning: Prune lightly in late winter or early spring by shortening main stems and side-shoots back to a good pair of fat buds. To rejuvenate older plants, prune a proportion of old stems almost to ground level in late winter.

Useful tips: Try growing this with a white-flowered clematis such as 'Duchess of Edinburgh'.

Flowering time: Late spring and early summer, and occasionally again in late summer.

Height: 1.8–2.4m (6–8ft)

Habit: Moderately vigorous, suitable for growing in confined spaces or containers.

Positioning: Best in light or moderate shade, as full sun tends to bleach the colour.

Care: Top-dress annually in spring with generous amounts of well-rotted manure. Deadheading and a summer feed of liquid general fertilizer will encourage a second crop of blooms late in summer.

Pruning: Train plants initially by pruning hard and spreading out resulting stems evenly to create a good framework. Prune each main stem lightly in late winter back to a good fat pair of buds.

Useful tips: Try growing this variety with a climbing rose such as 'Danse du Feu'; also successful in large containers.

A lovely variety with delicate colouring that shows up best in shade. The 15cm (6in) blooms are lightly scented, and produced in large quantities early in the season, followed often by a lighter second crop.

Very popular as a reliable, easily grown variety, with a more dependable colour and flowering season than the slightly paler 'Nelly Moser'. It is one of the best striped clematis, with the spring and summer blooms reaching 20cm (8in) in diameter, making a stunning display.

Flowering time: Late spring and early summer, and again in early autumn.

Height: 1.8–3m (6–10ft)

Habit: A strong-growing, vigorous variety that climbs well; the leaves are large and fairly sparse.

Positioning: Full sun or shade are suitable, the colouring being intensified in shaded positions. Very good on a sunless wall or in a dark corner.

Care: Top-dress with a good mulch of well-rotted manure every spring; feed during summer with a liquid general fertilizer every fortnight to encourage a second crop of flowers.

Pruning: Prune young plants hard at first and spread out stems evenly as they develop. Prune each main stem lightly in late winter back to a pair of fat buds.

Useful tips: This variety grows well on a dark background such as an ivy-covered wall, or with other paler clematis.

Flowering time: Mid- or late summer to mid-autumn.

Height: 1.8–2.4m (6–8ft)

Habit: Strong, vigorous growth, dying down to the ground after the autumn frosts, although a few stems may survive the winter in mild districts. Smooth, grey-green foliage.

Positioning: Full sun: shade encourages leafy growth. An open position sheltered from winds is beneficial. Ideal for mixed shrub borders, large pots.

Care: Mulch generously in autumn with well-rotted manure. Check for mildew in summer, and spray with a systemic fungicide.

Pruning: If any stems survive the winter, prune them hard back to about 30cm (12in) above ground level in early spring. Shorten excessively vigorous stems that may grow higher than normal without flowering.

Useful tips: Try growing plants at the foot of climbing roses to cover up their bare stems.

An exciting variety that usually dies down completely in winter, avoiding any necessity for pruning. The flowers are extremely elegant, like 5cm (2in) tulips in various shades of pink, produced continuously over quite a long season.

Often described as a climber, this is a hybrid between herbaceous C. *integrifolia* and the large-flowered climber C. x *jackmanii*. The intense 10–12cm (4–5in) indigo blooms are produced continuously over a long season, making this a particularly rewarding clematis for any garden. It looks stunning when grown through grey-leaved shrubs.

Flowering time: Early or mid-summer to early or mid-autumn.

Height: 1.2–1.8m (4–6ft), sometimes more.

Habit: Robust and erect semi-herbaceous shrub with non-clinging stems and narrow leaves up to 15cm (6in) long.

Positioning: Full sun or light shade, preferably with support, or near another shrub that it can scramble through, supported against injury from winds.

Care: An easy and reliable plant. Mulch well with well-rotted manure in autumn, and during the flowering season feed every fortnight with liquid general fertilizer. Tie in stems as they develop or make sure they are securely trained.

Pruning: Shorten branches by half in spring to produce a taller shrub in sheltered positions, or cut back all growth in autumn or winter.

Useful tips: Excellent for growing in a large container, provided it has sufficient support.

Flowering time: Mid-summer to early or mid-autumn.

Height: Up to 3m (10ft)

Habit: Slightly sprawling semi-woody shrub with slender stems. Small, unobtrusive leaves.

Positioning: An adaptable variety that thrives in full sun or light shade without any loss of colour. Plants are best given some kind of support from adjacent shrubs or a framework to which they can be tied.

Care: If grown on wires or trellis, stems need tying in regularly as they grow. Manure well in autumn and feed occasionally during the flowering season with a liquid general fertilizer.

Pruning: Stems often die back in winter; cut down any that survive almost to ground level, in spring or in autumn when plants are mulched.

Useful tips: Provided it has some kind of support, this is an ideal variety for growing in a large container. Combines well with heathers and dwarf conifers.

One of the easiest shrubby clematis to grow, and very rewarding, providing a continuous display of nodding dark violet to lavender flowers, 5cm (2in) across and shaped like flared bells.

Introduced by Jackmans as a tribute to the head gardener at Gravetye Manor, this robust *viticella* is normally not difficult to grow, and pruning is likely to be the only attention needed in most seasons. The glowing petunia-red flowers have an attractive velvety sheen.

Flowering time: Mid-summer to mid-autumn.

Height: Up to 4.5m (15ft)

Habit: One of the strongest-growing large-flowered clematis, very vigorous, with plenty of healthy foliage.

Positioning: Full sun for prolific flowering, which declines the colder or shadier the site. Very striking in a prominent position, preferably very open to reduce the incidence of mildew.

Care: Easy to grow in the right position. Generally disease-free and very resistant to wilt, but mildew can be a problem on a sheltered site. An occasional spray with systemic fungicide from mid-summer onwards is advisable.

Pruning: Hard pruning in late winter or early spring produces numerous flowers; prune lightly for fewer but larger flowers.

Useful tips: In mild areas harder pruning will be more appropriate, whereas light pruning is best in cold gardens.

Flowering time: Late spring to early summer.

Height: 1.8–2.4m (6–8ft)

Habit: Vigorous and bushy, flowering prolifically early in the season (with no autumn repeat).

Positioning: Any aspect is suitable, in full sun or light shade.

Care: No special care needed apart from a good mulch of well-rotted manure in spring.

Pruning: Minimal. In late winter or early spring cut out any dead and spindly shoots, and then tidy the rest of the growth, shortening each main stem back to the topmost pair of fat buds.

Useful tips: Sufficiently neat growth for growing in a container, perhaps with another later-flowering clematis to create a long season of colour. Like all blue varieties, combines well with another bright-coloured clematis, and also with white-flowered climbing roses.

Blue-flowered clematis have an appeal of their own, and this variety is one of the most enchanting. The deep mid-blue topsides of the 15–18cm (6–7in) blooms, with dark blue veins, contrast with their light blue reverse and the red-tipped white anthers. Blooms make good cut flowers.

'Etoile Violette'

This *viticella* hybrid is so free-flowering that the blooms seem to pile in masses on top of each other, completely hiding the foliage. The reddish-purple blooms are 8–10cm (3–4in) across, with a matt textured surface and contrasting creamy yellow stamens.

Flowering time: Early summer to early autumn.

Height: 3–3.6m (10–12ft), sometimes more.

Habit: Vigorous and very free-flowering over a short season.

Positioning: Full sun or dappled shade. A very versatile variety for growing as a specimen on walls, training on shrubs and climbing roses, and for combining with small ornamental trees.

Care: Hardy and disease-resistant; needs little special care. Every few years cut some of the old stems of taller plants back to about 30cm (12in) above ground level.

Pruning: Prune hard in late winter or early spring, back to a leaf joint just above the base of last year's growth, or to about 30cm (12in) above the ground.

Useful tips: Try growing with a yellow rose, 'Maigold' for example, or a pink variety such as 'Pink Perpétue'. Also looks good scrambling through the crab apple 'Golden Hornet'.

Flowering time: Late summer to mid-autumn.

Height: 4.5–6m (15–20ft), less if pruned hard.

Habit: Extremely vigorous, with strong twining vines, densely tangled, and neat glossy green leaves.

Positioning: An exuberant climber that can cope with full sun or shade. Best grown on buildings or large hedges or trained into trees.

Care: No special attention needed; established plants flower well even without annual dressings of manure or fertilizer. Train early growth carefully to avoid an impenetrable tangle of stems later.

Pruning: Prune hard in late spring to keep within bounds; or leave to ramble at will through shrubs and trees or over buildings.

Useful tips: Many plants are raised from seed, with variable results, so try to see your plant in flower before buying.

An energetic clematis that deserves its popularity. The flowers, although often less than 2.5cm (1in) across, are produced in billowing frothy masses and are followed by attractive seedheads. Its great glory is the perfume, which is powerful, heady and sweet, rather like that of hawthorn.

The simple species is a lovely plant but very rarely offered. This double form, with flowers like greenish-cream rosettes, is the variety usually grown. Rows of petals unfurl gradually, often over 2–3 weeks, and each bloom can take as long again to die, layer by layer. (syn. *C. f.* 'Flore Pleno', *C. f.* 'Plena'.)

Flowering time: Early summer to mid-autumn, later in warmth indoors.

Height: 1.8–3m (6–10ft)

Habit: Spindly open growth, with elegant stems; glossy leaves often remain semi-evergreen.

Positioning: May be grown on a warm sheltered wall, but in most regions best kept in large pots and moved into a frost-free greenhouse or conservatory for the winter. Or grow under glass all year.

Care: Make sure the soil is free-draining, train plants on a warm wall and protect them in winter with sheets of fleece draped over the stems and secured on all sides.

Pruning: If top growth is not killed in winter, cut off faded blooms back to a pair of strong buds as soon as flowering ceases. Otherwise cut down all growth in late winter or early spring to within 30cm (12in) or so of the ground.

Useful tips: It will often flower until early or mid-winter in warmth under glass.

Flowering time: Early summer to early autumn, or later under glass.

Height: 1.8–3m (6–10ft)

Habit: Slender and wiry, with an open habit and sparse foliage, bright green and shiny.

Positioning: Needs the shelter of a warm wall in very mild areas. Otherwise grow in containers for housing in frost-free conditions in autumn, or grow permanently under glass.

Care: Bring plants in pots under cover before first frosts. Grow outdoor plants in well-drained soil against a warm sheltered wall and cover with fleece in winter.

Pruning: Cut all top growth almost to ground level in late winter or early spring. Stems that survive the winter can be lightly pruned to produce taller plants.

Useful tips: This variety seems to have been developed from *C. f.* 'Alba Plena': whole plants or single stems sometimes revert to that form.

Sometimes known as the 'Passion Flower Clematis' because of the conspicuous purple boss of petal-shaped stamens at the centre of each 8–10cm (3–4in) bloom. As flowers first fade they often lose their outer petals, leaving this purple crown for several more days. (syn. *C. f.* 'Bicolor', *C. f.* 'Sieboldiana'.)

Very popular because of its tidy growth and reliability, this is one of the best introductions of the past two decades. The flowers are normally about 15cm (6in) across, but sometimes reach 20cm (8in) and are borne profusely in almost any position.

Flowering time: Early and mid-summer, sometimes continuing into late summer.

Height: Up to 2.4m (8ft)

Habit: Vigorous and strong-growing, but with an overall compact shape.

Positioning: A very reliable variety for any aspect in full sun or shade; does not fade in sun but often looks richer planted on a shady wall.

Care: Quite undemanding. There is a tendency to wilt, especially after damage to the stems, so make sure all growth is tied in securely to prevent loosening in winter winds.

Pruning: Prune lightly immediately after flowering, trimming off all spent flowers just above a strong pair of buds; a few stems may be pruned hard in late winter or early spring to induce later flowering.

Useful tips: Combines well with climbing roses which its compact growth is unlikely to smother.

Flowering time: Late spring and early summer, usually with a repeat in early autumn.

Height: 1.8–2.4m (6–8ft)

Habit: Very compact bushy growth, so especially suitable for restricted spaces.

Positioning: Any aspect, in full sun or lightly shaded, especially where the early blooms can be seen to advantage. Looks well in formal situations and also scrambling on drab hosts such as conifers.

Care: Quite undemanding. Feed liberally during early training. Mulch annually in spring with garden compost or well-rotted manure.

Pruning: Little needed, apart from hard initial cutting back to establish a bushy system of branches. If plants become straggly, cut right back to produce plenty of new stems.

Useful tips: This may be grown with a climbing rose to provide colour before the host plant comes into bloom. Also excellent for container cultivation.

Widely available and yet strangely neglected, this is one of the loveliest early flowering hybrids, its large star-shaped blooms glowing with a delicate beauty. Although pure white in some aspects, the crimped petals usually have a hint of violet at the edges.

'Gravetye Beauty'

The flowers maintain the typical *texensis* tulip shape for a few days and then open to slim-pointed stars that face skywards, their satiny surface gleaming with a rich lustre. With its glorious shade of rich cherry-red, this variety stands out spectacularly against a white wall. (Do not confuse with 'Gravetye', syn. 'Gravetye Variety', which is a *tangutica* hybrid.)

Flowering time: Mid- or late summer to early or mid-autumn.

Height: 1.8–2.4 (6–8ft), occasionally up to 3m (10ft).

Habit: Moderately vigorous, dying down to ground level in a hard winter. The leaves are smooth, bluish-green and well divided.

Positioning: Full sun, on a warm wall or in association with other climbers and tall shrubs, with shelter from cold winds. May also be grown over prostrate shrubs.

Care: Mulch well in autumn to protect the roots and ensure revival should all the top growth die back. Watch carefully for mildew and spray immediately with systemic fungicide.

Pruning: All growth is best pruned back to about 30cm (12in) in late winter or early spring.

Useful tips: Plants trail attractively over a groundcover rose such as 'Grouse' or can be trained on a once-flowering climber like 'Cécile Brunner' to follow on as the roses fade.

'Guernsey Cream'

Flowering time: Late spring and early summer, and again in late summer.

Height: 1.8–2.4m (6–8ft)

Habit: Moderately vigorous and compact, size and shape are easily controlled.

Positioning: Thrives in sun but the blooms achieve their best colouring only in semi-shade; grow as a highlight on a shaded wall, or in pots.

Care: The main branches should be carefully trained, to prevent their becoming tangled. Mulch in spring with well-rotted manure, and after the first flush of bloom dies down feed regularly until late summer.

Pruning: Prune lightly in early summer, cutting off all the faded blooms to a pair of good buds; in late winter or early spring shorten main stems and side-shoots back to two buds.

Useful tips: Excellent for growing in a large pot or small tub, and ideal for growing up a white climbing rose like 'Climbing Iceberg'.

Yellow is not a colour associated with large-flowered hybrids: of the few that exist this is the best, with its charming pale creamy yellow blooms that become almost white as they fade. Shade is almost essential for best effect, and even there the delicate colouring is sometimes tinged with green.

Justly popular for its ease of cultivation and free-flowering nature, this handsome hybrid has 10–15cm (4–6in) flowers which open a rich shell pink but may fade pleasantly in full sun. Flowering is almost continuous, but the size of the blooms varies according to the pruning method and season.

Flowering time: Early summer to early autumn.

Height: 1.8–2.4m (6–8ft)

Habit: Vigorous but compact, and often sparse. Very free-flowering.

Positioning: Full sun or light shade, but flowers fade in sunlight, so better grown on a lightly shaded wall. Dramatic in a large pot.

Care: Undemanding. Manure well in spring.

Pruning: Plants flower equally well on both young and old wood. Cut back close to the base of the previous year's growth in late winter or early spring to produce prolific smaller flowers in late summer and early autumn. If lightly pruned, very large blooms appear from late spring onwards, with smaller blooms spasmodically for the rest of the season.

Useful tips: May be combined with another clematis such as blue-flowered 'Perle d'Azur', or with a climbing rose like 'Compassion'; effective growing through a wall-trained *Ceanothus*.

Flowering time: Late spring and early summer, and again in late summer or early autumn.

Height: 1.8–2.4m (6–8ft), sometimes much more.

Habit: Moderately vigorous with dense, easily trained growth and solitary leaves that are large and leathery.

Positioning: Full sun or light shade: ideal for brightening up a partially shaded wall or corner.

Care: Generally trouble free but may suffer from wilt. Plant 8–10cm (3–4in) deeper than normal and tie in growth firmly as it develops, to prevent wind-rock damaging the stems. Drench the ground around plants once or twice each season with systemic fungicide.

Pruning: Prune lightly after flowering, cutting each dead bloom back to a pair of strong buds; or cut back hard in late winter or early spring, close to the base of the previous year's growth.

Useful tips: The flowers are ideal for cutting.

This is one of the oldest large-flowered hybrids in existence, and still widely grown as a favourite white variety. There is just a hint of cream in its 15–18cm (6–7in) flowers, which resemble tissue paper when lit from behind by the sun. Deserves a prominent position to display its classic beauty.

As true a mid-blue as may be found in any clematis, the large shapely flowers, up to 20cm (8in) in diameter, cover the plant evenly from top to bottom. Each petal has a soft pink central bar that quickly fades as the bloom opens.

Flowering time: Late spring and early summer, and again in early autumn.

Height: 2.4–3m (8–10ft)

Habit: Vigorous, bushy plant of moderate height, with evenly spaced foliage.

Positioning: Thrives almost anywhere, but prefers sun to shade, with some shelter from strong cold winds. Looks good on an old brick wall, and also the ideal choice for containers.

Care: An easy-going trouble-free variety. Manure well with well-rotted manure in spring, and train out main branches as they grow to prevent entwining.

Pruning: Minimal. Simply cut off the old flowers as soon as the season finishes, trimming them back to a pair of strong buds.

Useful tips: A good choice for growing with a pink or yellow climbing rose. For a really exciting combination, plant in a half-barrel with a rose such as 'Golden Showers' or 'New Dawn'.

Flowering time: Mid-summer, sometimes very late summer, until late autumn.

Height: 3–4.5m (10–15ft)

Habit: An exceptionally vigorous scrambler that will colonize large shrubs and small trees, or cover an old wall.

Positioning: Best planted in a warm sunny spot to ensure maximum flowering. The blooms face upwards, so allow plants to ramble over shrubs or a large hedge where the flowers can be enjoyed nearer ground level.

Care: Very easy to grow, hardy and disease-free. Mulch with garden compost in spring.

Pruning: Cut the stems back in late winter or early spring to near the base of the previous year's growth. However, some gardeners find that light pruning after flowering induces heavier flowering.

Useful tips: Normally grown on its own, but it will combine successfully with other plants.

An attractive but indecisive *viticella*, neither large- nor small-flowered, and often uncertain when to begin blooming: once it does start, however, it flowers continuously until the first frosts. One of the most vigorous white varieties. (syn. *C. x huldin.*)

This is a selected form of the plain species *C. integrifolia*, but with much larger flowers – at just over 5cm (2in) long, they are the largest in the group. As they age, their tapering sepals twist to reveal the furry creamy yellow anthers tightly packed in bundles.

Flowering time: Mid- and late summer.

Height: 60–75cm (2–2½ft)

Habit: Herbaceous and non-clinging, producing stems that are sometimes upright but more often trailing.

Positioning: Any aspect is suitable, with shelter from strong winds. Grow as a border plant, singly or in small groups, or allow to scramble over prostrate shrubs.

Care: Plant between other strong shrubs for support, and enclose groups with a few twiggy sticks to discourage sprawling. Top-dress annually with a mulch of well-rotted manure.

Pruning: Plants naturally die back in winter; cut and clear the dead stems, then mulch with manure.

Useful tips: If grown at the base of a climbing plant, lightly prune after flowering. Propagation is easy: dig up mature clumps at pruning time for division, or cut small portions with a spade from the side of the clump.

Flowering time:	Mid- and late summer.
Height:	60–75cm (2–2½ft)
Habit:	Herbaceous non-climbing growth, forming a thick clump of stems, sometimes self-supporting but otherwise weak and sprawling.
Positioning:	Full sun or light shade, preferably out of the wind; as single specimens or in groups of three, at the front of a border or the foot of roses, between upright shrubs or trailing over prostrate plants.
Care:	Very hardy and easy to grow. Mulch in early spring with well-rotted manure or garden compost. Provide some support in the form of twiggy sticks, especially in exposed borders.
Pruning:	Cut all the dead stems back almost to ground level in late winter or early spring.
Useful tips:	Allow the stems to trail across the ground or over prostrate roses like 'Nozomi'. Also grows well at the foot of a climbing rose, using it as a support.

One of the loveliest herbaceous plants, and very simple to grow and prune. The 5cm (2in) flowers are slightly perfumed and hang like nodding bells, the clear bright pink petals charmingly crimped and twisted. The several other varieties in this group are equally useful around the garden.

'Jackmanii Alba'

This is more than just a white form of the single purple 'Jackmanii' that everyone knows. The 12cm (5in) double flowers appear first on older stems, and vary in colour between light grey and pale bluish-lilac; they are followed by a prolific crop of large single blooms. (syn. *C. x jackmanii* 'Alba'.)

Flowering time: Early and mid-summer, and again in late summer and early autumn.

Height: 3–4.5m (10–15ft), sometimes more.

Habit: Very robust, the vigorous stems sporting masses of pale green foliage. Each bloom carries a distinctive ring of leaves part-way down its stalk.

Positioning: Almost any position, sunny or shaded.

Care: Provide stout support for the heavy foliage. Mulch generously in spring with garden compost or well-rotted manure, and watch out for mildew from late summer onwards.

Pruning: For masses of large single blooms, hard prune in late winter or early spring, cutting back near to the base of the previous season's growth. For double flowers prune after flowering, trimming faded blooms off just above a pair of strong buds.

Useful tips: Grow next to a large foliage shrub or on a large hedge.

Flowering time: Mid-summer to early autumn, sometimes up to a month earlier or later.

Height: 2.4–3m (8–10ft), often more.

Habit: Very vigorous leafy growth, with strong stems easily spreading to cover an area 1.8m (6ft) or more wide. Very free-flowering; the blooms often cover the foliage entirely.

Positioning: Thrives in full sun or light shade. Strong sunlight is best avoided as the colour can fade quickly.

Care: Mulch generously with garden compost or well-rotted manure in spring, and support the heavy growth securely on a strong framework.

Pruning: Cut back all stems in late winter or early spring almost to the base of the previous season's growth, and just above a leaf joint.

Useful tips: Try growing with two other complementary clematis like *C. campaniflora* (pruned hard) and herbaceous *C. integrifolia* 'Tapestry'.

An improved form of perhaps the most popular hybrid ever raised, and the one usually offered as 'Jackmanii'. Its large rich reddish-purple flowers make a strong statement wherever it is grown, especially when combined with other contrasting plants. (syn. *C.* x *jackmanii* 'Superba'.)

A lovely summer variety, the large star-shaped 20cm (8in) blooms invite closer inspection of their lightly crimped petals and their beautiful satin lustre. In some kinds of light the colour is a fascinating blend of pale grey and rich reddish-pink, in others a clear lilac with deeper edges and central bar.

Flowering time: Early or mid-summer, to late summer.

Height: 1.8–2.4m (6–8ft)

Habit: Moderately vigorous, almost restrained growth and a quite compact shape.

Positioning: Sun or light shade; the intensity of the colour changes according to the aspect. Some shelter from wind is preferred. Ideal for small gardens and for containers.

Care: Train plants evenly over the supports to make a balanced framework if they are to be pruned lightly. Top-dress liberally in spring with garden compost or well-rotted manure.

Pruning: Prune lightly after flowering, cutting back faded blooms to a strong pair of buds; or cut hard back in early spring almost to the base of last year's growth.

Useful tips: Try growing with a climbing rose that flowers at the same time – fragrant apricot 'Meg', for example – for an exciting early colour combination.

Flowering time: Mid-summer to mid-autumn.

Height: 1.8–3m (6–10ft)

Habit: Very vigorous, non-climbing annual growth from a permanent framework of woody branches. The large divided leaves assume purple or golden-yellow tints in autumn.

Positioning: Full sun or light shade. Very versatile: it may be grown as a shrub or lax climber, or as dense ground cover.

Care: Very hardy. Mulch lavishly in spring with garden compost or well-rotted manure. If grown as a climber, tie in the non-clinging stems as they grow.

Pruning: Either prune hard, cutting all growth back in late winter to about 30cm (12in) high, or prune to remove flowering stems and leave the woody stems untouched.

Useful tips: Ideal for trailing down a bank, or for covering a tree stump or fence. May also be grown on another shrub and over prostrate conifers.

This variety starts flowering earlier than the very similar x *jouiniana*, with a season that is about a month longer. Individual blooms are small and simple, but they appear in great masses, often smothering the foliage and giving the impression of a lovely blue mist.

'Lady Betty Balfour'

This *viticella* is one of the last clematis to flower each year. Its 12cm (5in) blooms, rich purple with contrasting creamy stamens, appear towards the end of the season, which makes it a valuable asset for late colour but also a difficult variety to site in cold gardens.

Flowering time: Early and mid-autumn, occasionally starting in late summer.

Height: 4.5–6m (15–20ft), sometimes less.

Habit: Extremely vigorous, producing masses of shoots not as densely covered in foliage as others of this type. Very free-flowering.

Positioning: In shade flowering starts late and is often curtailed by frost, so grow in a sunny warm position to encourage earlier blooms with fuller colour. Needs plenty of room, on a high wall, or planted with tall host plants.

Care: Top-dress in spring with plenty of garden compost or well-rotted manure, and train in the growth over the summer to achieve an even spread.

Pruning: Cut back exhausted growth in late winter or early spring almost to the top of the old wood, and just above a leaf joint.

Useful tips: An ideal companion for a tall climbing rose like the creamy white 'Mme Alfred Carrière'.

'Lasurstern'

Flowering time: Late spring and early summer, and again in early autumn.

Height: 2.4–3m (8–10ft)

Habit: Strong growth of moderate vigour, bushy and trouble free.

Positioning: Sun or shade, but the deep colour fades more quickly in full sun. Best on a lightly shaded wall or combined with other plants that cast a little protective shade.

Care: Mulch well with well-rotted manure in spring. Train out stems evenly as they develop, and feed at regular intervals after the first flush of bloom to ensure a reasonable autumn display.

Pruning: Trim off the faded blooms just beyond a good pair of buds. In early spring remove any dead or weak stems and lightly tip back the remaining growth to a pair of fat green buds.

Useful tips: Grow with a yellow climbing rose or train through a large rhododendron. Ideal for pergolas.

This is popular for its handsome and lavish display of 15cm (6in) deep-blue flowers that hold themselves well and almost obliterate the foliage in late spring. The later crop is more modest unless plants are pruned hard early in the season.

Flowering time: Mid- and late spring.

Height: 2.4–3m (8–10ft)

Habit: Very hardy and moderately vigorous, with slender stems covered in down while young, and prettily divided ferny leaves that open with the flowers.

Positioning: Any aspect, including an exposed shaded wall. Ideal for smaller walls, fences and archways, and for providing colour early in the year.

Care: Undemanding and totally weatherproof. Top-dress annually in spring with well-rotted manure or garden compost.

Pruning: Little or no pruning required after the initial framework is trained, but some gardeners prefer to trim all side-shoots almost back to their base after flowering.

Useful tips: Try to see plants in flower before buying, as most stocks are seed-raised and therefore variable. Excellent with a perennial sweet pea.

A favourite species for its early flowering and total reliability. The drooping double blue flowers open in huge masses at the same time as the elegant leaves start unfolding. After flowering, plants develop fluffy seedheads that last well into winter.

Flowering time: Mid- to late spring.

Height: 2.4–3m (8–10ft)

Habit: Hardy slender growth of moderate vigour, and fresh attractive foliage.

Positioning: Very hardy and will tolerate any aspect without injury or diminished flowering. A fairly restrained plant for low walls and fences or for training on a pillar.

Care: Little special care needed. Mulch well in spring with garden compost or well-rotted manure.

Pruning: Leave most of the plant unpruned to ensure plenty of seedheads, which are a special feature. Shorten one or two old stems annually after flowering to renew lower growth, or shorten all side-shoots after flowering to tidy the plant.

Useful tips: It also combines effectively with other similar species such as the plain *macropetala* and *alpina* 'White Moth', all flowering together.

Slightly smaller-flowered than the parent species, but no less lovely for that. The blooms look stunning *en masse* and cover the plant quite dramatically. Very happy in cool shade and similarly uninviting positions.

An open simple flower of airy *viticella* grace that appears smaller than its true size, 10–12cm (4–5in) across. In full bloom, however, an established plant is a stunning sight and recognizably one of the best red varieties, the colour remaining bright and clear throughout the season.

Flowering time: Mid-summer to early autumn, often starting earlier.

Height: 2.4–3m (8–10ft)

Habit: Very vigorous growth forming a compact mass of healthy foliage. Flowers over an unusually long period.

Positioning: Full sun or light shade. A little shade helps display the colour to best effect. Sufficiently compact for growing on pillars or in containers.

Care: Almost totally resistant to wilt. An easy variety, ideal for beginners. Manure generously in spring.

Pruning: Cut back all the top growth hard in late winter or early spring to about 30cm (12in) above the ground, or to just above the base of last year's growth.

Useful tips: May be allowed to scramble over low-growing plants such as a bed of white roses, but also looks good trained over taller shrubs or hugging the trunk of a tree.

'Margot Koster'

Flowering time: Mid-summer to early autumn.

Height: 2.4–3.6m (8–12ft)

Habit: Very vigorous, with large rounded foliage that makes an effective dark foil for the informal blooms.

Positioning: Any aspect, lightly shaded or in full sun; flowers show good resistance to fading in bright sunlight. Their colour has more impact at a distance, so position at the end of a path or across a lawn.

Care: Plants are very hardy, almost completely resistant to wilt and simple to maintain. Mulch lavishly in spring with garden compost or well-rotted manure.

Pruning: Cut down all growth in late winter or early spring, either to about 30cm (12in) high or to just above the base of last year's stems if this is higher.

Useful tips: An asset in any garden and position. Planted against a dark hedge at the bottom of the garden, its impact in full flower is arresting.

This has unusually large blooms for a *viticella* and is often listed as a large-flowered hybrid. It is so free-flowering that plants can present a solid wall of eye-catching colour, even though the curled and reflexed 10cm (4in) flowers have a very open appearance individually.

'Marie Boisselot'

Perhaps the best-known white clematis and justifiably so, for its impact is unforgettable. Its enormous 20cm (8in) satiny blooms have a delicate fragrance and appear almost continuously over a long season wherever it is planted, even in semi-shade. (syn. 'Mme Le Coultre', 'Mevrouw Le Coultre'.)

Flowering time: Early summer to early autumn.

Height: 3–3.6m (10–12ft), sometimes much more.

Habit: Strong-growing with large plentiful foliage that makes an effective backdrop to the steady succession of blooms.

Positioning: Any aspect is suitable, full sun or shade, but often looks most impressive on a shady wall. Do not let it grow too high, as the blooms face upwards.

Care: An easy and vigorous variety. Mulch well in spring with well-rotted manure. Watch out for mildew on late flowers and spray with systemic fungicide at the first signs.

Pruning: Cut back hard in early spring to produce a prolific late display in autumn. For very large early blooms, prune lightly immediately after flowering, or combine both methods for a long season of colour.

Useful tips: Train over low or medium-sized bushes such as rhododendrons or shrub roses.

Flowering time: Mid-summer to early autumn.

Height: 3–3.6m (10–12ft)

Habit: Strong healthy growth forming a leafy compact shape. Its leaves are larger and more rounded than the species.

Positioning: Full sun or light shade. A naturally agile climber, best on a wall or a pergola, or trained into a small tree.

Care: A tough hardy variety with good disease resistance. Top-dress in spring with garden compost or well-rotted manure.

Pruning: Prune hard in late winter or early spring, cutting all growth back to about 30cm (12in) above the ground or to just above the origin of the previous year's stems.

Useful tips: One of the best for training up an old apple tree, an ornamental crab like 'Echtermeyer' or 'Wisley', or a lively climbing rose such as 'Climbing Shot Silk' or 'Climbing Bettina'.

This particularly attractive and award-winning *viticella* has small flowers like its parent, about 5cm (2in) across, that appear without flagging over a full three-month season. Individual blooms are worth close examination for their delicate shading from ivory white to rich rosy purple.

A first-class large-flowered clematis, well liked and still highly recommended 130 years after its introduction. The attractively shaped blooms, 12cm (5in) across, have a relatively short season but appear prolifically in a great dramatic rush early in the year.

Flowering time: Late spring and early summer.

Height: 1.8–2.4m (6–8ft)

Habit: Moderately vigorous, making a fairly compact leafy plant that bushes out in a satisfying way on all sides.

Positioning: Any aspect, sunny or shaded; full sun produces dense satiny white petals with a cream central bar, whereas in shade the earlier blooms have a pale green bar and a hint of pink.

Care: Undemanding, disease free and easy to grow. Mulch in spring with well-rotted manure, and feed after flowering.

Pruning: Trim faded blooms back to just beyond a pair of strong buds. In early spring, cut out dead or spindly growth and shorten stems to the topmost pair of fat green buds.

Useful tips: A good choice for container cultivation. Looks well on a climbing rose or planted against a dark evergreen background.

montana 'Marjorie'

Flowering time: Late spring and early summer.

Height: 6–9m (20–30ft)

Habit: Exuberant growth that needs plenty of room. Develops into a dense tangle of stems unless pruned firmly each year. The foliage is pale green and shapely.

Positioning: Choose sites carefully as plants never look their best if cramped. Avoid shade and plant on a large sunny wall sheltered from cold winds.

Care: On dry or impoverished soils a spring mulch of well-rotted manure is beneficial, otherwise plants often flower well without annual feeding.

Pruning: Immediately after flowering trim all side-shoots back almost to their origin, and also shorten long invasive stems.

Useful tips: A hard winter may suppress flowering, so avoid frost hollows and full exposure to cold winds. An ideal variety for disguising a large eyesore or for growing into tall trees.

This fairly recent hybrid (1980) makes a very large plant, even in terms of the naturally rampant vigour of most *montana* varieties. The semi-double flowers look uninspiring when they first open but quickly develop their full creamy pink colouring, in a mass display that can last 8 weeks or more.

The latest-flowering *montana*, often starting 2–4 weeks after other varieties (although when first introduced the original plant was described as autumn-flowering). The creamy white 5cm (2in) blooms have a distinctive spidery appearance and a scent similar to that of chocolate. (syn. *C. m.* 'Wilsonii'.)

Flowering time: Early and mid-summer.

Height: 9m (30ft)

Habit: Possibly the most vigorous of all *montana*s. The flowers are borne in great profusion.

Positioning: Any aspect. Site with care: garden walls, archways and pergolas may easily be swamped, and it can penetrate roofs and gutters. Perhaps best on a tree, where it can scale great heights. In cold gardens some shelter is advisable.

Care: Little required apart from pruning. Mulch rarely except on very dry soils or where plants are restricted.

Pruning: Plants naturalized in large trees may be left unpruned. Elsewhere trim all side-shoots back to their base and shorten long invasive shoots. In smaller spaces trim again in late winter.

Useful tips: Try growing this as ground cover in a large bed, training the stems over the first few years to radiate over an area of 6sq.m (65sq.ft).

'Mrs N Thompson'

Flowering time: Late spring and early summer, and again in early autumn.

Height: Up to 1.8m (6ft)

Habit: Not very vigorous, and benefits from solid support. Shapely but rather sparse foliage.

Positioning: Any aspect. A little daily sunshine will enhance the colour, but full sunlight can prematurely fade blooms. Provide some shelter from cold winds.

Care: Support from adjacent shrubs or a post or pillar helps plants reach full size. Mulch generously in late winter with garden compost or well-rotted manure, and give regular feeds after early flowers until autumn buds are about to break. Very susceptible to wilt, so treat early signs promptly.

Pruning: Light pruning immediately after flowering is best.

Useful tips: Grow over low shrubs, or against the bare stems of tall climbing roses. Effective in a container.

This modest variety is irresistible, especially just after the 12cm (5in) flowers first open. Their fresh colouring is a lively violet-purple with a rich velvet sheen and a conspicuous central bar of bright red. As time passes the colour fades softly to a matt elegance.

'Mrs P B Truax'

Among the first blue-flowered clematis of the season, the satiny-textured blooms, 15cm (6in) across, open at first with a green central bar down each petal. Blooms later fade from periwinkle blue to a refreshing paler shade.

Flowering time: Late spring and early summer, with a few flowers occasionally in autumn.

Height: Up to 2.4m (8ft)

Habit: Moderately vigorous with well-balanced growth and enough large leaves to produce a satisfying compact bush.

Positioning: Most aspects are suitable provided plants receive sunlight for at least half the day. A good variety for a wall or pillar.

Care: Plants are robust and easy to grow. Top-dress annually in spring with garden compost or well-rotted manure. Feed regularly to encourage late blooms.

Pruning: Cut off faded blooms just beyond a pair of strong buds. In late winter or early spring remove any dead or weak growth and tidy strong stems back to the topmost pair of large green buds.

Useful tips: An excellent variety for growing in containers.

'Multi Blue'

Flowering time: Late spring and early summer, and again late summer and early autumn.

Height: 1.8–2.4m (6–8ft)

Habit: Moderately vigorous, producing a compact bushy plant that is slow to reach its full size.

Positioning: Thrives in any aspect, although sunlight for at least part of the day enhances the unusual colour.

Care: No serious problems provided it is fed well, both during initial soil preparation, and afterwards annually in spring with a mulch of well-rotted manure. Give extra feeds during the following season.

Pruning: Cut off faded blooms back to a strong pair of buds. In late winter or early spring cut out any dead and weak growth, and then trim main stems back to the top pair of fat green buds.

Useful tips: A fine variety for a large container, especially when combined with bold summer bedding.

A fairly modern variety, introduced in the 1980s as a sport from 'The President' and rapidly proving popular for its dual flowering season and unusual appearance. The semi-double blooms open a layer at a time, to produce a central crown of narrow spiky petals.

Flowering time: Late spring and early summer, and again in early autumn.

Height: 2.4–3m (8–10ft)

Habit: Very vigorous, rapidly growing as wide as it is high. Large fresh green foliage. Very free-flowering.

Positioning: Thrives in any situation, but full direct sunlight fades the colour and plants succeed best in semi-shade.

Care: Early training is important. Prepare the ground thoroughly before planting and then top-dress annually in spring with well-rotted manure.

Pruning: Prune lightly after flowering by cutting off all the faded blooms just beyond a strong pair of buds. Some branches on established plants may be cut hard back in spring to rejuvenate growth.

Useful tips: Try growing over large wall-trained shrubs, especially those such as *Garrya elliptica* that are comparatively dull when the clematis is in flower.

This was introduced exactly a century ago and for much of the time since has been one of the best-known varieties, with a reputation for reliability, vigour and prolific flowering. Its only problem is that the colour of the 20cm (8in) blooms can fade rapidly in sunlight, but careful siting will easily prevent this.

'Niobe'

Flowering time:	Early summer to early autumn.
Height:	1.8–2.4m (6–8ft)
Habit:	Moderately vigorous restrained growth resulting in a compact bushy plant, flowering steadily and almost continuously.
Positioning:	Almost any aspect, in full sun or light shade, is acceptable, but sunlight for at least part of the day is advisable to do full justice to the colour. Its neat compact growth makes it ideal for containers.
Care:	Very easy and undemanding to grow. Mulch annually with well-rotted manure. Feed with a general fertilizer at mid-summer.
Pruning:	Prune hard in late winter or early spring to produce a brilliant autumn display, or prune lightly after flowering for an early summer start, continuing until the autumn.
Useful tips:	Makes an effective partner for a climbing rose or another (taller) clematis such as 'Gipsy Queen'.

A modern award-winner from Poland that has become one of the most sought-after red clematis. The star-shaped blooms, 15cm (6in) across at first but later in the season 10cm (4in), are a sultry deep ruby initially, changing gradually to a lively bright red, enhanced by the conspicuous creamy stamens.

The result of a cross between two very handsome parents, *C. viticella* and *C. texensis* 'Etoile Rose', which explains both its restrained growth and the fragile beauty of its 6cm (2½in) bell-shaped blooms. The charming reflex of the pointed petals produces the effect of a pagoda roof.

Flowering time: Mid-summer to early autumn.

Height: 1.8m (6ft)

Habit: Moderately vigorous, with slender stems that can appear weak and spindly. The foliage is small and attractive.

Positioning: Full sun or light shade. Choose a position where its delicacy is seen to advantage.

Care: Needs little special care. Prepare the soil well before planting, and mulch generously each spring with well-rotted manure. A mid-summer feed of general fertilizer just before the first buds open can be beneficial.

Pruning: Cut back hard in late winter or early spring. Prune away all top growth annually about 30cm (12in) above the ground.

Useful tips: Try growing it to cover the lower half of another clematis such as a more vigorous *viticella*, or let it trail down a bank or over a low wall. Also looks effective scrambling over heathers and prostrate conifers.

Flowering time:	Early summer to early autumn.
Height:	3–4.5m (10–15ft)
Habit:	Very strong plants with vigorous stems. The foliage is bright and plentiful, though almost totally obscured by the flowers.
Positioning:	Any aspect, sunny or shaded, is suitable and plants are free-flowering even on sunless walls.
Care:	Young plants often suffer from wilt, but recover after treatment to become vigorous specimens. Mulch annually in spring with well-rotted manure, and feed at mid-summer with a general fertilizer.
Pruning:	Cut down all growth in late winter or early spring to about 30cm (12in) above ground. Taller plants can be encouraged by training stems and lightly pruning after flowering.
Useful tips:	A perfect bedfellow for a wisteria, sharing similar colouring and extending the flowering season.

Extremely popular throughout its long life (it was introduced in 1885) for the unbroken succession of blooms that blanket plants in startling profusion. The slightly nodding flowers, 12cm (5in) across, are individually quite plain, but it is the massed impact that always provokes comment.

'Peveril Pearl'

The pearly lustre of its petals sets this variety apart from other pale lilac clematis. There are two distinct flushes of bloom; the first has very large 20cm (8in) flowers while those appearing in autumn are smaller. All have the enchanting quality of changing their colour according to the light.

Flowering time: Late spring to early summer, and again in early autumn.

Height: 1.8–3m (6–10ft)

Habit: Moderately vigorous, with strong stems producing a compact bushy plant. Very free-flowering.

Positioning: Some shade as the colour tends to fade in sun. Ideal for dark corners and shaded walls. Provide shelter from strong winds.

Care: Prepare the soil thoroughly and top-dress annually in spring with plenty of well-rotted manure. After the first flush of blooms, feed once or twice with a general fertilizer to stimulate a good second crop.

Pruning: Train to establish a balanced framework. Thereafter prune lightly, trimming faded blooms back to a pair of strong buds. In late winter cut out dead and spindly growth and tidy main stems back to the topmost pair of fat buds.

Useful tips: An excellent variety for container cultivation.

Flowering time: Early summer and again in early autumn.

Height: 1.8m (6ft)

Habit: Moderately vigorous, but often slow to establish and build up a framework of stems. Produces a compact plant with restrained foliage.

Positioning: Sun or shade, but its colour is best seen in filtered sunlight or against a pale background. Ideal for walls, and containers.

Care: Prepare the ground thoroughly and mulch annually in spring with well-rotted manure. Train patiently in the early stages while stems are developing. Once plants are flowering well, feed with a general fertilizer at mid-summer.

Pruning: Minimal. When flowering finishes, cut off all faded blooms just above a pair of strong buds.

Useful tips: Try combining with cream-coloured climbing roses or a pink shrub rose such as 'Gertrude Jekyll'.

A very old variety, still popular with gardeners for its softly romantic blooms that resemble 15cm (6in) double peonies early in the season. The later flowers have a simple and memorable charm, especially when displayed in good light.

An exceptionally showy species that finally won awards long after its introduction a century ago. The nodding flowers resemble tiny bells, at first a charming primrose yellow and later fading to parchment, with a seductive scent of cowslips. (syn. *C. nutans* hort.)

Flowering time: Mid-summer to early autumn.

Height: Up to 6m (20ft)

Habit: Often slow to establish. A dense bush of short growth for the first few seasons, before developing into a strong climber with large hairy leaves.

Positioning: Sun or shade, but full sunlight encourages plants to flower earlier and continue well into autumn.

Care: Prepare the ground thoroughly and mulch annually in spring with well-rotted manure for the first few years; thereafter plants often thrive without further feeding.

Pruning: To cover a large area of wall or hedge, or to climb into a tree, prune lightly after flowering. Otherwise prune hard in late winter for more restrained growth.

Useful tips: To appreciate the flowers at close quarters, cut back every spring to 30–60cm (12–24in), and fan out the young stems on a wall or fence.

'Rouge Cardinal'

Flowering time: Mid-summer to early autumn.

Height: 1.8–2.4m (6–8ft)

Habit: Moderately vigorous with strong stems, but producing a compact plant of modest height.

Positioning: Any aspect, in full sun or shade, although the rich colour is more intense and slower to fade on a shaded wall. An ideal subject for containers.

Care: Hardy and trouble free. Manure generously in spring and feed with a general fertilizer in late summer. Container plants will need feeding every fortnight.

Pruning: Cut back all growth in late winter or early spring almost to the origin of the previous year's stems and just above a leaf joint. Occasionally cut one or two older stems to 30cm (12in) high to rejuvenate growth.

Useful tips: Eye-catching grown on its own on a pillar or against a pale wall.

A rival for 'Niobe' as the best red clematis, although there is a tendency for flowers to fade noticeably from their initial rich burgundy colour to a deep cerise. The 12cm (5in) blooms have a fine depth of colour and a satiny sheen.

The strong rich purple of this award-winning variety amply merits its name. The 15cm (6in) blooms are fully double in the earlier flush, with conspicuous pale bars and contrasting veins, whereas the autumn flowers are simple and almost luminous in their intensity.

Flowering time: Early to mid-summer, and again in early autumn.

Height: 1.8–2.4m (6–8ft)

Habit: Vigorous and strong-growing, but making a very compact tidy plant with attractive leaves.

Positioning: Full sunlight for at least half the day is essential. The exceptionally compact habit makes this suitable for small gardens where space is limited. Provide some shelter from strong cold winds.

Care: Mulch annually in spring with well-rotted manure. Often affected by wilt in its early years, but responds to careful fungicidal treatment.

Pruning: Early pruning aims to build up a strong system of stems, which are then pruned lightly after flowering by trimming off all the faded blooms just beyond a strong pair of buds.

Useful tips: Perfect for containers, especially if combined with another (mid-season) variety.

'Royal Velours'

Flowering time: Mid-summer to early autumn.

Height: 3–3.6m (10–12ft)

Habit: Very vigorous with strong exuberant stems and plenty of small neat foliage.

Positioning: Grows happily in any position, but best in at least partial sunlight where the colour is seen at its best.

Care: Robust, and trouble free. Mulch annually in spring with garden compost or well-rotted manure.

Pruning: Prune hard in late winter or early spring, cutting all growth back to about 30cm (12in) above ground level, or just above the base of the previous year's growth if this is higher.

Useful tips: Lends itself to dramatic companion planting. Try growing it with the honeysuckle *Lonicera japonica* 'Halliana', pruned hard at the same time, together with orange-flowered *Eccremocarpus scaber*. Pyracanthas and flowering crab apples are other complementary hosts.

The single *viticella* flowers are barely 5cm (2in) across, and yet plants flower with such abandon that the overall impact is breath-taking. Depending on the light, flowers appear velvety red or almost purple, always with a lustrous satiny sheen.

A very satisfying flower with an overall colour that can be pale mauve or lavender according to aspect, but always with distinct silver-grey overtones and a wonderful satiny sheen. The 12cm (5in) blooms may appear in two distinct flushes or continuously in a steady sequence.

Flowering time: Late spring and early summer, and again in late summer, or continuous throughout.

Height: 1.8–2.4m (6–8ft)

Habit: Very vigorous, with strong healthy growth producing a compact bushy plant. Large shapely foliage.

Positioning: Sun or shade, but the colour shows best in a shady corner or against a dark wall. Sufficiently compact for growing on a pillar or in containers.

Care: Feed liberally in the early stages while building a framework of stems. In following seasons mulch annually in spring with garden compost or well-rotted manure.

Pruning: Simply trim the side-shoots back to a strong pair of buds immediately after flowering, or cut back hard to 30cm (12in) high in late winter or early spring.

Useful tips: For maximum impact grow this on a 1.5m (5ft) tripod in a large container in a shaded corner of a patio.

'Sunset'

Flowering time: Early summer to late summer, sometimes until later.

Height: 1.8–2.4m (6–8ft)

Habit: Very strong and robust, making vigorous growth and producing a neat compact plant with bushy foliage.

Positioning: Full sun or light shade, although the intense colour is most effective on a shaded wall. Good for small gardens and containers.

Care: An undemanding plant. Top-dress annually in spring with garden compost or well-rotted manure. If there is a break in flowering, feed with a general fertilizer until later flower buds swell.

Pruning: Light pruning is best, cutting all faded blooms back to a pair of strong buds. Hard pruning in late winter, cutting back to just above the origin of last year's stems, will result in a larger crop of late flowers.

Useful tips: A good variety for combining with an early-flowering climbing rose.

A fairly modern introduction from the USA, notable for the almost fluorescent glowing colour of its prolific blooms, 10–12cm (4–5in) across and borne in large numbers on the sturdy stems. The satiny contrasting central bar down each petal and the bright yellow anthers add strong highlights to the flowers.

'Tage Lundell'

Like all its relatives, this is one of the toughest types of clematis, with a robust constitution hidden beneath the grace and charm of the lovely solitary blooms. Occasionally a few late flowers appear among the prominent fluffy seedheads that last well into winter.

Flowering time: Mid- to late spring, sometimes again in early autumn.

Height: 1.8–2.4m (6–8ft)

Habit: Fairly vigorous with slender stems and very attractive foliage divided into many toothed leaflets.

Positioning: All aspects, and plants tolerate exposure and poorer soils.

Care: Good drainage in winter is important. Make sure the soil is open and porous, working plenty of grit and similar coarse material into heavy ground. On poor soils mulch annually in spring with garden compost.

Pruning: Prune after spring flowering – trim side-shoots of wall-trained plants back to about 15cm (6in) long; other plants can be cut back to about 60cm (2ft) high.

Useful tips: Try combining with climbing roses to flower while their stems are still bare. Also shows up well against a yew hedge or on a small bay tree.

tangutica

Flowering time: Mid-summer to mid-autumn.

Height: 3–4.5m (10–15ft)

Habit: Strong wiry stems that grow vigorously despite hard pruning, with dense prettily divided foliage and long-stemmed blooms.

Positioning: Happy in most situations sheltered from cold winds. Tolerates shade well but flowers best with sunlight for at least part of the day.

Care: Undemanding provided the drainage is good – work plenty of grit or other coarse material into heavy soil before planting. On poor ground mulch annually in spring with well-rotted manure.

Pruning: Cut back hard in late winter or early spring, almost to the base of the previous year's growth and just above a leaf joint.

Useful tips: Almost all plants are grown from seed and are therefore variable – try to see specimens in flower before buying, or choose a named form like 'Aureolin'.

Best known of all the yellow-flowered species and often called the citrus-peel clematis (although that name properly belongs to the very similar *C. orientalis*). The small nodding flowers, only 2.5–4cm (1–1½in) long, resemble buttercup-yellow lanterns and are followed by silver seedheads that shine in the sun.

Over a century old and deservedly still a great favourite. A bold and very prolific variety, with full star-shaped blooms 18cm (7in) across that may appear in two main flushes or very often in a continuous display over the full season.

Flowering time: Late spring to early autumn.

Height: 1.8–3m (6–10ft)

Habit: Very vigorous with strong stems and large foliage, bronze-purple tinted when young and later dark green.

Positioning: Any aspect, sunny or shaded, is suitable; plants bloom well on shady walls, while in full sun the colour resists fading.

Care: Easy and undemanding. Mulch lavishly every spring with well-rotted manure.

Pruning: Once stems have been trained, little or no pruning is required. Trim faded blooms back to a pair of strong buds, and then tidy plants in spring by removing dead and spindly growth.

Useful tips: Combines impressively with a climbing rose such as 'Galway Bay', 'Mermaid' or 'Schoolgirl', and also with a sturdy open shrub or small tree, *Cytisus battandieri* for example.

Flowering time: Late summer to mid-autumn.

Height: 4.5–6m (15–20ft)

Habit: A very strong, vigorous climber with long wandering stems and smooth pale leaves divided into numerous leaflets.

Positioning: Sun or shade, although the flowers look most effective in full sun.

Care: A very easy variety. Ensure good winter drainage, and allow plenty of room for the vigorous growth. Mulch annually in spring with garden compost to retain moisture.

Pruning: Cut back hard in late winter, close to the base of the previous year's growth and just above a leaf joint. May also be left unpruned where it is growing inaccessibly in a tree.

Useful tips: To achieve a full cascade of bloom on the long stems, limit the height of supports to about 3m (10ft). Ideal for growing beside a seat to appreciate the fragrance.

A choice hybrid produced more than a century ago by the famous clematis specialist Jackman. Its simple flowers, edged with wine-red and possessing a fascinating scent of almonds, are only 5cm (2in) across but appear in huge numbers like billowing clouds. (syn. *C. flammula* 'Rubromarginata')

'Venosa Violacea'

An unmistakable hybrid with some of the largest blooms in the *viticella* group, 10cm (4in) across and very distinctive with the depth of colour at the sepal margins contrasting boldly with the central white bars.

Flowering time:	Early summer to early autumn.
Height:	2.4–3m (8–10ft)
Habit:	Vigorous with strong stems and large leaves.
Positioning:	Any aspect, sunny or lightly shaded, is suitable, but the rich colour shows up best in good light against a pale wall.
Care:	Hardy and disease resistant. Mulch in spring with well-rotted manure.
Pruning:	Cut back hard in late winter or early spring, about 30cm (12in) above the ground or close to the base of the previous year's growth to encourage plenty of new stems from low down.
Useful tips:	The unobtrusive foliage allows this variety to blend well with all kinds of shrubs as host. May be combined with orange- or apricot-coloured shrub roses, or with a rambler such as 'Ethel'.

lowering time: Early summer to early autumn.

Height: 2.4–3m (8–10ft), sometimes much more.

Habit: Very vigorous, with strong stems and large healthy foliage.

Positioning: Full sun or shade suits this variety, which excels on a shady wall where the rich colours show up strikingly.

Care: Undemanding. Plants are very hardy, disease resistant and easy to grow. Mulch lavishly in spring with well-rotted manure, and feed in late summer with a liquid general fertilizer.

Pruning: In late winter or early spring, cut back all stems hard almost to the base of the previous year's growth and just above a leaf joint.

Useful tips: For a stunning partnership train into a small specimen of the white-berried mountain ash *Sorbus cashmiriana.* Also very effective combined with climbing roses.

A vivacious Jackmanii type that can be relied on to provide plenty of colour late in the season, when all stages of growth are displayed simultaneously: the large pendent buds, freshly opened nodding blooms that are a rich rosy purple, and older flowers fading to a soft elegant lilac.

Although classed as a *viticella* hybrid, its mysterious parentage is known to include the semi-herbaceous *C. texensis*. This variety does not die back in winter, though, and if pruned lightly will eventually festoon quite large trees. Justifiably popular for its vibrant colour and long season.

Flowering time: Mid-summer to mid-autumn, sometimes starting much earlier.

Height: 3–9m (10–30ft) according to pruning.

Habit: Very vigorous growth that makes a tall vine. If not pruned hard annually, lower stems become bare and gaunt. Fresh green and shapely foliage.

Positioning: Any aspect, although best where it receives direct sunlight for at least half the day.

Care: Easy to grow and almost completely disease resistant. Shortage of water or nutrients causes browning and lower leaf loss. Mulch lavishly in spring with well-rotted manure.

Pruning: Cut back hard in late winter or early spring to limit the height to 3m (10ft), pruning all growth back almost to the point of origin. Light pruning after flowering will encourage taller plants and earlier flowering.

Useful tips: Grow it through a host shrub or an evergreen hedge.

Flowering time: Late spring and early summer, and again in late summer.

Height: 2.4–3m (8–10ft)

Habit: Very vigorous strong stems that produce a compact shapely plant with handsome foliage.

Positioning: Sun or shade, but the vivid colouring is most intense in some sunlight. Shelter from strong winds to protect the early blooms.

Care: Easy to grow and very robust. Mulch generously each spring with well-rotted manure. One or two supplementary feeds of liquid general fertilizer at mid-summer will encourage late flowering.

Pruning: Prune lightly immediately after flowering, cutting all faded blooms back to a strong pair of buds. Alternatively prune hard in late winter or early spring to stimulate a more impressive late flush of blooms.

Useful tips: One of the best new varieties for growing in a large container.

A very new variety (introduced from Denmark in 1993) that is already making a name for itself because of the depth of colour of its 18cm (7in) blooms and its free-flowering habit. The flowering season may be modified according to the pruning method chosen.

'Vyvyan Pennell'

The result of crossing two famous varieties, 'Daniel Deronda' and 'Beauty of Worcester', this is one of the classic clematis, available everywhere. There are two distinct seasons: a very early flush of fully double 12cm (5in) flowers, and another in autumn of luminous large single blooms up to 20cm (8in) across.

Flowering time: Late spring and early summer, and again in early autumn.

Height: 1.8–2.4m (6–8ft)

Habit: Vigorous and strong-growing, often making a dense plant as wide as it is tall against a wall. The foliage is large and handsome.

Positioning: Full sun or light shade, but the first flowers may open too early in full sun, resulting in injury from frost and cold winds.

Care: Mulch annually in spring with well-rotted manure. Shelter plants from late spring frosts or cover with fleece against hard weather. Susceptible to wilt and young plants will need fungicidal treatment to recover.

Pruning: Prune lightly immediately after flowering, cutting all faded blooms back to a pair of strong buds.

Useful tips: Do not grow on a brick wall or wooden fence, as the colour can look dingy against a dark background. An effective partner for an evergreen shrub.

'Wada's Primrose'

Flowering time: Late spring and early summer, with an occasional bloom in autumn.

Height: 1.8–3m (6–10ft)

Habit: Moderately vigorous, with numerous slender wiry stems bearing heart-shaped leaves and making a bushy plant.

Positioning: Although plants flower in sun or shade, the delicate yellow fades rapidly in strong light. The best position is a shaded corner.

Care: Plants may be slow to establish. Top-dress generously in spring with a mulch of well-rotted manure. Supplementary feeding after the early blooms fade will help strengthen the new flowering growth.

Pruning: Little or no pruning is needed. Train and shape growth as it develops and cut off all the old blooms back to a pair of strong buds.

Useful tips: Try growing on a dark shaded wall, or in the dappled sunlight of woodland shrubs.

Some authorities consider this to be the same variety as 'Moonlight', while others identify distinct differences: both have also been sold as 'Yellow Queen'. This is the nearest to a yellow large-flowered clematis yet produced, although the colour is more a pleasing soft cream with a pale primrose stripe. Early flowers are often tinted green.

'White Swan'

Flowering time: Mid- to late spring.

Height: 1.8–2.4m (6–8ft)

Habit: Very hardy, robust constitution, tolerating harsh weather and producing compact plants with neat attractive foliage.

Positioning: Thrives in any aspect, sunny or shaded, although plants seem happiest in cool shade. An ideal choice for an open shady wall.

Care: No special care necessary. Ensure good drainage, and top-dress with well-rotted manure every spring. In its first couple of years train a firm even framework of branches.

Pruning: Tidy after flowering by trimming the side-shoots of wall-trained plants to within a couple of buds of the main branches. Plants may be left unpruned, except for one or two main stems which can be cut back almost to ground level after flowering to induce new growth.

Useful tips: Any climbing rose is an ideal partner.

Variously described as an *alpina* or a *macropetala*, this is in fact a hybrid between the two, with larger blooms than either species. The double flowers, often up to 12cm (5in) across, tend to be a very soft creamy colour rather than pure white.

This book belongs to

This book belongs to

Bluebell Glade

Dandelion Dell

Heart of Misty Wo[od]

Hawthorn Hedgerows